A Guide To Marriage For Men - Quotes

Rabbi Zevi Wineberg

DEDICATION

Dedicated to Our Loving Creator for the eternal gift of marriage!

ACKNOWLEDGMENTS

I humbly acknowledge Chassidus – Jewish mysticism and particularly the first Chabad Rebbe, upon whose concepts found in this book the guide is based.

A Guide To Marriage For Men; Quotes

"So you are both attracted and frightened; attracted by the force of your wife's personality yet repelled by her tongue."

.
.

"Women; you can't live without them, but you can't live with them."

"The truth is that the Lubavitcher Rebbe, Rabbi Menachem Mendel Schneersohn, the greatest scholar of our times - and the greatest Kabbalist - explains, that because today it is so very important for there to be peace in the home, the Satan puts his utmost effort into destroying marriages."

"Let's face it, no one wants to be shouted at, so the big question is do we desire it or not."

·

·

"The answer lies in understanding the purpose of marriage."

·

·

·

"I have a brother who is part scholar, part psychologist, and I once asked him about marriage, and he told me something profound - He said, "It is not natural for man and woman to be together, but that is what G-d desires and thus …" well he didn't finish the sentence, but if I may ... "thus we do it."

.

.

"However marriage must be understood for the reason why G-d desired it! and then we can suffer – and in fact THRIVE through it."

.

"They say there are three rings, the engagement-ring, the wedding-ring, and the suffer-ring :)"

.

.

"But in all seriousness when we understand that marriage is meant to be just that, a challenge of personal growth, then it all becomes a joyous journey."

.

.

"It says, that when Adam received his wife he found, "an assistance, opposing him."

Now this is a very strange term, what is an assistance, opposing?

If it is assistance it is not opposing; if however it is opposing, it is not an assistance?!

The answer is that when man is perfect, then his wife is an assistance, for she assists his noble endeavors; However if man is a selfish narcissistic creature, then she opposes him.”

.

.

“**Kabbalistickly, man comes from the right side of the sefiros [kabbalistic levels] which includes a predilection to love and kindness, while the woman is from the left side, which is a predilection toward fear and *Din*.**”

“**Now *Din* is a very important concept in our marital therapy booklet, *Din* means for lack of a better translation: judgment.**”

•

"A woman is always judging if something is fair or not.

That's why women keep score of points differently from men."

•

•

"As a man is about *Chessed* - love and giving, if he buys his wife an expensive diamond ring, he thinks he scored big - for there was a lot of

sacrifice and love that went into that expensive gift.

However Din looks at it differently, "if you gave me a diamond, than I owe you something in return."

Din does not see all the time, effort, money, and love, rather Din is simply a scale; if you weighed a diamond, it is about the same weight say as a salad or chicken, so "the salad I make for you, or the chicken I serve you, is the equivalent of a diamond."

"Now this is where marital intimacy is so important, because a man can give his wife <u>pleasure</u> and it is a lot of pleasure, therefore he can score big."

.

.

"However there is something far deeper that goes on in marital intimacy and in romantic love [not lust,] which is why it is so valuable to a woman, and he can be forgiven for all his "sins.""

[Remember Din is all about fairness, and so even if you

weren't bad, but by not giving as much as she, you were bad!]

At the heart of Din comes the preceding emotion which is anxiety.

The reason someone gets into Din is because they are anxious about being ashamed.

And thus they figure, by acting appropriately they are on safe ground – in other words, when a person is happy they don't mind giving even to someone who doesn't deserve it - however if a person - for example is feeling oppressed, then they will only give in a reciprocal fashion."

.
.

"So the key is what is called in Kabbalah *hamtakas hadinim* "sweetening [or in marital terms, 'romantic'izing'] the judgments."

"So by a man caring for – taking his wife out… – eliminating her fears, meaning being a true *"knight in shining armor,"* then the woman feels secure, and she stops counting [again this is all in her head - which is why men can't understand what frustrates women] and she in turn begins to give unconditionally."

.

.

"So this is the great trick: to go the extra romantic mile, and then the woman will stop counting / Din, and react with unconditional love."

"Of course most men are not really capable – or should I say inclined – to do this, for the simple reason, that they are selfish."

.

.

"When we say men are inclined to love and giving, it usually means they are inclined to loving themselves and giving to themselves and thus as long as they have a rush in trying to win over the woman they are dating etc. they are giving, however this giving is not giving at all, it is really taking.

In other words if you woo an

investor to your company and you buy him drinks etc., are you giving to him or are you really taking from him? The answer of-course is that you are only loving yourself; the proof is, if he didn't have any money to offer you, you wouldn't be wooing him nor spending a red dime on him."

.

.

"So here is where men lose it, that they are exceptional, and try hard to win a woman through great romantic strides, however once they have the woman, and they are satisfied; because they never really cared about her – she was only a means for themselves – thus they stop giving, and then the women who by nature is Din orientated, and believes in justice, in commitment, in love, in a lasting relationship! ends up giving more, and ends up resenting the fact that she is giving so much, and not getting anything in return."

.

.

"And this concludes this short booklet but perhaps the most insightful one you will ever read on the subject

for it brings us back to the Biblical statement: "If you are deserving, then your wife will be an assistance in your personal journey of growth in a manner of the likes that no one in the world will give to you, for Din does give everything in return!"

.

.

"However if like most men, you are basically selfish, then you can expect that after a while, Din will judge you for it, and then will begin to express anger and frustration and perhaps a

bit of verbal venom [or a lot of it…] for Din has decided that you need to shape up."

.
.

"The trick to a happy marriage – if you can't motivate yourself to do the right thing and romanticize you wife – is to understand that she is merely fulfilling her mission in life. – She is not opposing you – she is maturing you, she is growing you! She is offering you the novel concept that Din has merit, that you <u>do</u> need to be just and fair, and you need to commit, even when you just

want to drink a beer and watch a football game;

In other words you need to become a real man."